D1487392

DISCARD

# Just the Opposite
# Hard / Soft

## Exactamente lo opuesto
## Duro / Blando

**Sharon Gordon**

**Marshall Cavendish**
Benchmark
New York

This apple is hard.

❖

Esta manzana es dura.

This apple is soft.

❖

Esta manzana es blanda.

This hat is hard.

❖

Este sombrero es duro.

This hat is soft.

❖

Este sombrero es blando.

This egg is hard.

❖

Este es un huevo duro.

This egg is soft.

Este es un huevo blando.

This ball is hard.

Esta pelota es dura.

This ball is soft.

❖

Esta pelota es blanda.

This candy is hard.

Este dulce es duro.

This candy is soft.

❖

Este dulce es blando.

This chair is hard.

❖

Esta silla es dura.

This chair is soft.

❖

Esta silla es blanda.

This cup is hard.

❖

Esta taza es dura.

This cup is soft.

❖

Esta taza es blanda.

This doll is hard.

❖

Esta muñeca es dura.

This doll is soft.

❖

Esta muñeca es blanda.

This ice cream is hard.

❖

Este helado es duro.

This ice cream is soft!

✦

¡Este helado es blando!

# Words We Know
## Palabras que sabemos

apple
manzana

ball
pelota

candy
dulce

chair
silla

cup
taza

doll
muñeca

egg
huevo

hat
sombrero

ice cream
helado

# Index

Page numbers in **boldface** are illustrations.

apples, **2**, 2–3, **3**, **20**

ball, **8**, 8–9, **9**, **20**

candy, **10**, 10–11, **11**, **20**
chair, **12**, 12–13, **13**, **20**
cup, **14**, 14–15, **15**, **21**

doll, **16**, 16–17, **17**, **21**

egg, **6**, 6–7, **7**, **21**

hard, 2, **2**, 4, **4**, 6, **6**, 8, **8**, 10, **10**, 12, 12, 14, 14, 16, 16, 18, 18
hat, **4**, 4–5, **5**, **21**

ice cream, **18**, 18–19, **19**, **21**

soft, 3, **3**, 5, **5**, 7, **7**, 9, **9**, 11, **11**, 13, **13**, 15, **15**, 17, **17**, 19, **19**

# Índice

Las páginas indicadas con números en **negrita** tienen ilustraciones.

blando/blanda, 3, 3, 5, **5**, 7, **7**, 9, **9**, 11, **11**, 13, **13**, 15, **15**, 17, **17**, 19, **19**

dulce, **10**, 10–11, **11**, **20**
duro/dura, 2, **2**, 4, **4**, 6, **6**, 8, **8**, 10, **10**, 12, **12**, 14, **14**, 16, **16**, 18, **18**

helado, **18**, 18–19, **19**, **21**
huevo, **6**, 6–7, **7**, **21**

manzana, **2**, 2–3, **3**, **20**
muñeca, **16**, 16–17, **17**, **21**

pelota, **8**, 8–9, **9**, **20**

silla, **12**, 12–13, **13**, **20**
sombrero, **4**, 4–5, **5**, **21**

taza, **14**, 14–15, **15**, **21**

## About the Author
### Datos biográficos de la autora

Sharon Gordon has written many books for young children. She has always worked as an editor. Sharon and her husband Bruce have three children, Douglas, Katie, and Laura, and one spoiled pooch, Samantha. They live in Midland Park, New Jersey.

Sharon Gordon ha escrito muchos libros para niños. Siempre ha trabajado como editora. Sharon y su esposo Bruce tienen tres niños, Douglas, Katie y Laura, y una perra consentida, Samantha. Viven en Midland Park, Nueva Jersey.

With thanks to Nanci Vargus, Ed.D.
and Beth Walker Gambro, reading consultants

Marshall Cavendish Benchmark
99 White Plains Road
Tarrytown, New York 10591-9001
www.marshallcavendish.us

Text Copyright © 2007 by Marshall Cavendish Corporation

All rights reserved. No part of this book may be reproduced or utilized in any form or by any means
electronic or mechanical, including photocopying, recording, or by any information storage and
retrieval system, without written permission from the copyright holders.

Library of Congress Cataloging-in-Publication Data

Gordon, Sharon.
Hard soft = Duro blando / Sharon Gordon. — Bilingual ed.
p. cm. — (Bookworms. Just the opposite)
Includes index.
ISBN-13: 978-0-7614-2448-2 (bilingual ed.)
ISBN-10: 0-7614-2448-2 (bilingual ed.)
ISBN-13: 978-0-7614-2368-3 (Spanish ed.)
ISBN-10: 0-7614-1571-8 (English ed.)
1. Matter—Properties—Juvenile literature. 2. Touch—Juvenile literature. 3. Polarity—Juvenile literature. 4. English
language—Synonyms and antonyms—Juvenile literature. I. Title. II. Title: Duro blando. III. Series: Gordon, Sharon.
Bookworms. Just the opposite (Spanish & English)

QC173.16.G6718 2007
530.4'12—dc22
2006017350

Spanish Translation and Text Composition by Victory Productions, Inc.
www.victoryprd.com

Photo Research by Anne Burns Images

Cover Photos: *Corbis*: (top-Theresa Vargo), (bottom-Robert Holmes)
The photographs in this book are used with permission and through the courtesy of: *Corbis*: pp. 1 left, 16, 21 (top left)
Rob Lewine; pp. 1 right, 17 Jose Luis Pelaez, Inc.; pp. 2, 20 (top left) Norbert Schaefer; pp. 4, 21 (top right) Jim Cummins;
p. 5 Bill Miles; pp. 7, 13, 18, 21 (bottom left) Royalty Free; pp. 8, 20 (top right) Scott Wohrman; p. 9 Kim Robbie;
p. 10 Theresa Vargo; pp. 11, 20 (bottom left) Robert Holmes; pp. 12, 20 (bottom right) Ariel Skelley; p. 14 Annie Griffiths;
p. 15 Owen Franken; pp. 19, 21 (bottom right) James Leynse/SABA. *SWA Photo*: pp. 3, 6.

Series design by Becky Terhune

Printed in Malaysia
1  3  5  6  4  2